Leaving My Homeland

A Refugee's Journey from Afghanistan

Helen Mason

Crabtree Publishing Company
www.crabtreebooks.com

Crabtree Publishing Company
www.crabtreebooks.com

Author: Helen Mason

Editorial director: Kathy Middleton

Editors: Sarah Eason, Kelly Spence, and Janine Deschenes

Design: Jessica Moon

Cover design: Jessica Moon

Photo research: Rachel Blount

Proofreader: Wendy Scavuzzo

Production coordinator and prepress technician: Ken Wright

Print coordinator: Margaret Amy Salter

Consultants: Hawa Sabriye and HaEun Kim,
   Centre for Refugee Studies, York University

Publisher's Note: The story presented in this book
is a fictional account based on extensive research
of real-life accounts by refugees with the aim to reflect the
true experience of refugee children and their families.

Written and produced for Crabtree Publishing Company
by Calcium Creative

Photo Credits:
t=Top, bl=Bottom Left, br=Bottom Right

Shutterstock: Asianet-Pakistan: pp. 25, 29; Brothers Good:
p. 6c; Frank Gaertner: p. 24b; Kafeinkolik: p. 23c; LOVE YOU:
pp. 5b, 27t; Macrovector: pp. 3, 6t, 13t, 14c, 22t, 24t; Svetlana
Maslova: pp. 20t, 23tl, 23b; MSSA: pp. 14t, 16b, 29tr; Teodor
Ostojic: p. 4; Lizette Potgieter: pp. 7b, 8b, 9; PremiumStock:
p. 8tr; Procyk Radek: p. 18; RedlineVector: p. 5tl; Seita:
p. 14–15b; Ken Tannenbaum: p. 10b; Sudtawee Thepsuponkul:
p. 27; Travel Stock: p. 6b; Jim Vallee: pp. 5t, 20b; What's My
Name: p. 10–11b; UNHCR: © UNHCR/Zsolt Balla: p. 19b;
© UNHCR/Insiya Syed: p. 16; © UNHCR/Aubrey Wade: p. 21;
© UNHCR/Gerhard Westrich: p. 19r; Wikimedia Commons:
Al Jazeera English (www.flickr.com/people/32834977@N03):
p. 11t; Master Sgt. Tracy DeMarco/U.S. Air Force:
p. 17t; ISAF Headquarters Public Affairs Office (www.flickr.
com/photos/29456680@N06) from Kabul, Afghanistan: p. 12;
Staff Sgt. Andrew Smith (U.S Army Photographer): p. 15b; S.K.
Vemmer (U.S. Department of State): p. 17b.

Cover: Shutterstock: Macrovector (right), Nadzeya Shanchuk
(bottom).

Library and Archives Canada Cataloguing in Publication

Mason, Helen, 1950-, author
    A refugee's journey from Afghanistan / Helen Mason.

(Leaving my homeland)
Includes index.
Issued in print and electronic formats.
ISBN 978-0-7787-3125-2 (hardcover).--ISBN 978-0-7787-3129-0 (softcover).--
ISBN 978-1-4271-1878-3 (HTML)

    1. Refugees--Afghanistan--Juvenile literature. 2. Refugee children--
Afghanistan--Juvenile literature. 3. Afghan War, 2001- --Juvenile literature.
4. Refugees--Social conditions--Juvenile literature. 5. Afghanistan--Social
conditions--Juvenile literature. I. Title.

HV640.5.A28M38 2017   j305.9'0691409581   C2016-907085-9
                                                      C2016-907086-7

Library of Congress Cataloging-in-Publication Data

Names: Mason, Helen, 1950- author.
Title: A refugee's journey from Afghanistan / written by Helen Mason.
Description: New York, N.Y. : Crabtree Publishing, 2017. |
  Series: Leaving my homeland | Includes index.
Identifiers: LCCN 2016054821 (print) | LCCN 2016059638 (ebook) |
  ISBN 9780778731252 (reinforced library binding : alk. paper) |
  ISBN 9780778731290 (pbk. : alk. paper) |
  ISBN 9781427118783 (Electronic HTML)
Subjects: LCSH: Refugees--Afghanistan. | Refugee children--Afghanistan. |
  Afghan War, 2001---Juvenile literature. | Afghanistan--Social conditions--
  Juvenile literature.
Classification: LCC HV640.5.A28 M38 2017 (print) | LCC HV640.5.A28 (ebook) |
  DDC 362.7/791409581--dc23
LC record available at https://lccn.loc.gov/2016054821

Crabtree Publishing Company

www.crabtreebooks.com   1-800-387-7650

Printed in Canada/102017/BF20170919

Published in Canada
Crabtree Publishing
616 Welland Ave.
St. Catharines, ON
L2M 5V6

Published in the United States
Crabtree Publishing
PMB 59051
350 Fifth Avenue, 59th Floor
New York, New York 10118

Published in the United Kingdom
Crabtree Publishing
Maritime House
Basin Road North, Hove
BN41 1WR

Published in Australia
Crabtree Publishing
3 Charles Street
Coburg North
VIC, 3058

What Is in This Book?

Leaving Afghanistan

For more than three decades, there has been conflict in Afghanistan. At times, wars have been fought between the country's different **ethnic** and religious groups. Other conflicts have involved foreign countries. Most recently, the United States and other **Western** nations were at war with Afghanistan. They were fighting against **terrorism** in the country.

Bombs have destroyed many Afghan towns and cities.

UN Rights of the Child

Every child has **rights**. Rights are privileges and freedoms that are protected by law. **Refugees** have the right to special protection and help. The United Nations (UN) Convention on the Rights of the Child is a document that lists the rights that all children should have. Think about these rights as you read this book.

Although the war officially ended in 2014, fighting has continued. Terrorism is still a problem. Soldiers from other countries remain in Afghanistan today.

The fighting has destroyed towns and cities. Millions of people have been forced from their homes because of the violence.

UZBEKISTAN

TURKMENISTAN

TAJIKISTAN

IRAN

Afghanistan

Afghanistan is in
the center of Asia.

PAKISTAN

Afghanistan's flag

ARABIAN SEA

Some people leave their **homeland** to look for better opportunities in other places. These people are **immigrants**. When Afghans are forced to flee their homes but remain in the country, they become **internally displaced persons (IDPs)**. Many other people have fled Afghanistan and become refugees in nearby countries. In 2015, there were more than 2.6 million Afghan refugees living outside of Afghanistan.

My Homeland, Afghanistan

Afghanistan has a long history. Pieces of human bone and tools that are 30,000 years old have been found in the country. Afghanistan was one of the first places where farming took place, and was home to one of the first civilizations.

Kabul

Kabul is the capital of Afghanistan.

A mosque is a Muslim house of worship.

Afghanistan has been a largely Muslim country since the 600s C.E. Muslims are people who belong to the Islamic faith. They follow the teachings of the prophet Muhammad.

During the 1970s, Afghanistan was **invaded** by the **Soviet Union**. In 1989, Afghan fighters drove the Soviets out. Different groups within Afghanistan then struggled for power.

In 1996, an **extremist** group of terrorists called the **Taliban** gained control of the country. They enforced very strict laws. Men were beaten if they did not go to mosque five times a day. Women could not work and they had to completely cover their bodies before leaving their homes. They also had to have a male relative with them when they were outside. Some Afghans thought these rules made the country safer. Unfortunately, they did not.

Afghanistan's Story in Numbers

Many different ethnic groups live in Afghanistan. More than half are Pashtun. The official languages of Afghanistan are Pashto, which is spoken by the Pashtun, and Dari.

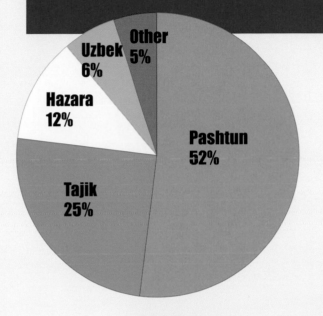

Other 5%

Uzbek 6%

Hazara 12%

Pashtun 52%

Tajik 25%

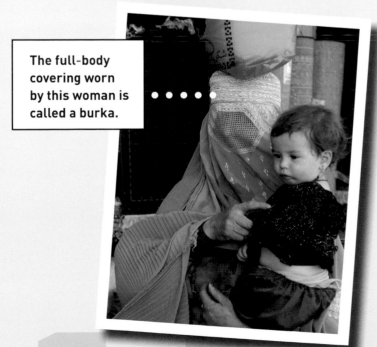

The full-body covering worn by this woman is called a burka.

Sonita's Story: Stories of Our Homeland

I am Pashtun. I was born in 2008 in Islamabad, the capital of Pakistan. I have never seen Afghanistan. My mother and father, Mora and Baba, have told me all about our homeland. I have also seen some pictures online and on our neighbor's cell phone.

My older brother Izat was born in Afghanistan. We also have a little sister named Hala. She was born in Pakistan. Our mother tells us stories about our homeland.

The *Attan* is a traditional Pashtun dance. Dancers often perform barefoot in colorful costumes.

Afghanistan is a very mountainous country.

Mora's Life Before the War

I grew up in eastern Afghanistan. I lived with my grandparents, parents, aunts and uncles, brothers and sisters, and many cousins. My family owned a large flock of sheep. When I was young, I went to the hills with my grandparents and uncle during the summer.

We lived in a tent made from poles and cloth. I helped Anaa, my grandmother, make and cook naan bread. I rolled the dough into flat circles, then watched it brown over the fire.

One fall, I returned to town with the sheep. I was excited to start school. But the Taliban had taken over the town. Girls could not go to school. I could not even play outside with my brother.

The next year, I fell and broke my arm. Anaa said I needed to see a doctor. But the Taliban had fired all the female doctors. And they would not let a man touch me. So Anaa set my arm. It is still a little crooked.

Afghanistan's Story in Numbers

In 2015, about **3.5 million** children living in Afghanistan did not go to school.

During the summer, many Afghan families move their herds of sheep into the mountains to graze.

The Afghan Conflict

While the Taliban was in power, other terrorist groups took shelter in Afghanistan. They shared similar extremist ideas about religion. One powerful group is called **al-Qaeda**. Members of al-Qaeda think that foreign armies should stay out of countries such as Afghanistan, even if they are there to help. They kill people who do not agree.

On September 11, 2001, four airplanes were taken over by terrorists. Two crashed into the World Trade Center in New York City. Another struck the Pentagon. A fourth plane crashed in Pennsylvania. Al-Qaeda was responsible for the attack. The United States government demanded that the Afghan government hand over Osama bin Laden, the leader of al-Qaeda. At the time, the Taliban ruled Afghanistan. They refused to hand over bin Laden.

Nearly 3,000 people were killed during the September 11 terrorist attack.

The United States declared war on Afghanistan. They invaded the country to remove the Taliban from power. There was more fighting. Many people were killed.

By December 2001, the Taliban no longer ruled Afghanistan. The Afghan people struggled to form a **democratic** government. After many years of conflict, it was difficult for people to agree. In 2004, the country elected a president. In 2009 and 2014, the country had two more elections.

Afghan soldiers patrol the roads to remove dangerous bombs left by terrorists.

Although the war ended in 2014, Afghanistan is still a very dangerous place to live. The Taliban continues to attack citizens, soldiers, and police. There are other terrorist groups in the country, too, such as the **Islamic State in Iraq and the Levant (ISIL)**. ISIL thinks that anyone who does not agree with their beliefs should be killed. This includes other Muslims. Many Afghans live in fear of terrorist groups.

UN Rights of the Child

You have the right to choose your own religion and beliefs.

Sonita's Story: My Family Leaves Kabul

Mora Continues

I married your Baba. At first we lived in Kabul. Then the foreign soldiers came.

There were lots of bombs. The noise was so loud. Afterward, there was dust everywhere and the smell of smoke.

With the Taliban gone, we had more freedom. Some women started a school for girls. I learned to read. I was so proud.

Then we had a son. We named him Izat. In 2006, he started school. I was so happy. My son would be educated.

The mountains provide hiding places for terrorists. An army patrol checks the road to keep it clear for refugees.

UN Rights of the Child

Every child has the right to live in freedom and dignity.

But bad things happened. Baba got a note from the Taliban. It said "Join us or we will kill you." Baba did not want to join the Taliban. He believed it was wrong to kill people.

If we stayed, the Taliban would kill him. So we left Kabul. We headed for Pakistan.

The army stopped our bus at a roadblock. Everyone had to get off. A soldier asked where we were going. Baba said we were going to visit family.

Afghanistan

Kabul

Islamabad

Pakistan

In Pakistan, we went to the capital, Islamabad. We lived in a mud hut outside the city. It was there our beautiful daughter was born. We named her Sonita.

SOS: We Need Help

The United Nations (UN) is an organization made up of many countries. It works to solve problems and help people in need. The UN has worked in Afghanistan for many years.

In 2001, several countries sent troops to help track down al-Qaeda and make Afghanistan safer. The UN and other organizations brought food and other supplies for the Afghans who had suffered under the Taliban government.

The UN also worked with Afghan leaders. They helped organize a temporary government to run the country. Foreign soldiers helped the new government establish laws and reopen schools. Today they remain in Afghanistan to help fight against terrorism.

Some aid organizations give Afghans in need kits that contain clothing, soap, cooking pots, and other items.

UN Rights of the Child

Your education should help you use and develop your talents and abilities. It should also help you learn to live peacefully, protect the environment, and respect other people.

There are many organizations in Afghanistan that help Afghans in need, too. Help the Afghan Children (HTAC) is a group that has worked in the country since 1993. HTAC partners with the Afghan government. Together they create school programs that teach children how to peacefully solve problems with others. HTAC also works with other aid organizations to provide food and aid to people in need. With its partners, the organization has helped more than 1.7 million Afghans.

Many organizations, such as HTAC, believe that teaching young Afghans how to solve problems without violence will help make the country peaceful in the future.

Life in a Refugee Camp

Many people who flee end up living in camps for IDPs and refugees. Each camp has a headquarters. Aid workers organize housing, medical care, and education. When Afghans arrive in a camp run by the UN, they register with the United Nations High Commissioner for Refugees (UNHCR). This means they put their names on an official list of refugees.

An Afghan family visits a UNHCR office in Pakistan. The UNHCR is the branch of the UN that helps refugees.

Many people arrive with nothing. They receive a blanket, a bucket, a place to live, and a **ration card**. The card is stamped when refugees pick up food. Sometimes rations are cut because there is not enough food for everyone.

Afghanistan's Story in Numbers

In 2016,
9.3 million
Afghans did not have a secure source of food.

Life in a camp is hard. The streets are dirty. There are no sewers. There is often no electricity or running water. It is very hot during the summer, and very cold during the winter. Proper winter clothing and heaters are needed to keep shelters warm.

In Farah province, in western Afghanistan, internally displaced families line up in a camp to receive warm clothes for the cold winter ahead.

In Afghanistan, the World Food Program gives extra food to people who work to learn new skills. People who learn a **trade** get vegetable oil. These skills can help refugees earn a living and provide for their families. Schools are also set up in some camps. Families receive vegetable oil for sending a girl to school.

Dr. Habiba Sarabi was a refugee in 1996. She taught girls in refugee camps in Pakistan and, in secret, in Afghanistan. In 2015, she became the first woman to govern an Afghan province. It is called Banyam province.

Sonita's Story: My Life in Kot Chandana

When I was two, my family and I moved to a refugee camp. Mora was going to have a baby. In the camp, we would be given food and shelter.

Baba, Mora, Izat, my little sister Hala, and I live in the Kot Chandana refugee camp. Our house is made of mud bricks. From the doorway, I can see mountains. I would like to climb those mountains some day.

Many children are born in refugee camps. Mothers receive extra food while caring for their babies.

For now, my life is here. I help Mora take care of Hala and I help with the housework. I gather firewood and carry water. The water cans are very heavy.

I need to do a lot of chores before school. I get up early. Baba and Izat get up early, too. Izat is learning to be a tailor to make clothes. Baba drives a **rickshaw** in a nearby village. Some days he gets a lot of work. He comes home happy. Other days, his pockets are empty.

A refugee named Aqeela Asifi started a school, similar to this one, at Kot Chandana. More than 1,000 girls have graduated from her school.

Afghanistan's Story in Numbers

1 in 5

Afghan children are born in a refugee camp.

Many children attend classes in refugee camps. They complete chores before school.

One night, Baba did not come home. I could not sleep. Mora stayed up all night. He came the next day. The police had put him in jail. They said he did not have permission to run a business. He showed them his registration card. But they did not believe him. They scared him, then let him go.

Some Countries Welcome Refugees

For many years, Afghan refugees have been fleeing to neighboring countries. The people in Pakistan and Iran have done a lot for them. But these countries are also experiencing conflict. It is difficult for them to house millions of refugees. More help is needed.

Iran hosted more than 950,000 Afghan refugees in 2015.

Iraq

Iran

Afghanistan

Pakistan

In 2015, Pakistan housed 1.6 million registered refugees. Two million more were unregistered.

UN Rights of the Child

You have the right to help
from the government if
you are poor or in need.

Other countries around the world gave money. But few wanted
to give homes to these refugees.

Some people do not want refugees living in their countries. They
are concerned that they might be a threat because they come
from places where terrorist groups are located. This fear of
Muslims is called **Islamophobia**. But Afghan refugees are
fleeing from war and terrorism, too. They need safe places
to live. Many refugees settle in Australia, Sweden, Finland,
and Norway, as well as in other countries.

This Austrian family
welcomed Nooria,
an Afghan refugee,
along with her
young daughter. In
Afghanistan, Nooria
worked for the UN.

Sonita's Story: My Uncle Goes to Europe

One day, Baba came home with a letter. It was from Uncle Noor, Mora's youngest brother. Baba shut the door before he started to read. He spoke in a whisper. We all gathered close to listen.

Sister,

Our father is dead. The Taliban have killed him. I wanted revenge. But mother said no. She went to a **smuggler.** She paid $6,000. "Do not come back," she said. "No matter how bad it gets."

The smuggler gave me travel papers. He took me by truck to Turkey. From there, I hid in a vegetable wagon. We traveled through the mountains for two days.

At the sea, the smugglers crowded too many people onto a boat. The boat was too heavy, and it sank off the coast of Greece. Many people drowned. I was lucky. Nice people saved me. I'm now in Germany. People are good to me here. But I worry about mother. Now, she is alone.

We were all crying when Baba finished reading the letter.

Afghanistan's Story in Numbers

In 2015,

88,300

child refugees traveling without parents applied for **asylum** in Europe. More than half of them were from Afghanistan.

In the first five months of 2016, 2,500 refugees drowned trying to reach Europe by boat.

Refugees travel by car, truck, train, bus, boat, plane, and on foot.

Challenges Refugees Face

It can be very difficult for refugees to understand the culture in a **host country**. Western and Afghan cultures are very different. People often dress and act differently. Many Afghan women wear a head scarf called a **hijab**, or other body coverings. Men do not look directly at women. It is considered disrespectful.

It can be challenging for adult refugees to find work in new countries. Many have to go back to school. Learning to speak and read a new language, such as English, can be difficult. Some refugees choose to become citizens of a new country. This sometimes offers a better future for refugees and their children.

For Dari speakers, it is difficult to learn English. In the Dari language, letters take different shapes depending on where they appear in a word.

Some Afghan refugees choose to return to their homeland. Since 2002, the UNHCR has worked with the Afghan government to create a **repatriation** program that brings refugees home from Pakistan. Refugees are given money to cover the costs of travel and settling down. Once in Afghanistan, the UNHCR helps people with housing, jobs, and medical needs.

Parts of the country are still very dangerous. Returning to Afghanistan brings many challenges for refugees. Afghans dream of the day when their homeland will be at peace.

The UNHCR provides transportation for Afghan refugees returning from Pakistan.

Afghanistan's Story in Numbers

In 2015, the UN helped almost

250,000

Afghan refugees return. In October 2016, about 7,400 refugees arrived in Afghanistan every day. Sixty percent were under the age of 18.

25

Sonita's Story: We Return to Afghanistan

Life became difficult in the camp. First, Baba disappeared. Members of the Taliban had attacked schools in Pakistan. The Pakistan government blamed Afghans for the attacks. It wanted all of the Afghan refugees to leave the country.

Baba was arrested. When the police let him go, he could not find work. Neither could Izat. It was no longer safe for us in Pakistan. Baba said we must go back to Afghanistan. There, he might be able to find work.

Mora and I were afraid to return to Afghanistan, but we understood that Baba and Izat needed to work to help us survive. So we packed.

Kabul

Afghanistan

Kot Chandana

Pakistan

UN Rights of the Child

Every child has the right to a name and a nationality.

The UN gave us $400 each. That is a lot of money. We could use it to find a new home.

Other people were leaving, too. The bus was crowded. It was filled to the ceiling with belongings.

When we arrived in Kabul, it did not look like the city from Mora's stories. There was damage from the war everywhere. I felt scared, but I was also excited to see my family's homeland.

Izat has a vegetable cart now. He makes $3 every day. That is enough to feed us. Baba works in construction. I am able to go to school. I feel very lucky. The best news is that I finally met my Anaa. We are grateful to have found her.

People can be in danger because of things left behind in war, such as explosive land mines. The UNHCR gives refugees returning to Afghanistan information to help them stay safe.

You Can Help!

There are many things that you can do to help people affected by the Afghan conflict, both in your community and around the world.

 Welcome people from other countries and cultures in your community.

 Research aid organizations that work in Afghanistan, such as UNICEF, and make a donation.

 Knowledge is powerful. Share what you have learned with others.

 Spread the word. Encourage others to do their part to help refugees in need.

 Organize an event, such as a walk, to draw attention to the Afghan refugee crisis.

 Show your support. With an adult's permission, search online for petitions to sign that support giving aid to Afghans in need.

 Research organizations in your community that help refugees. Get in touch and see how you can help.

Afghanistan's Story in Numbers

In 2017, the US government donated

$1.25 billion

to assist refugees and development in Afghanistan.

HUMANITARIAN
AID

Protesters demand a stop to terrorism in Peshawar, Pakistan.

Discussion Prompts

1. How do you think an Afghan child who has grown up in Pakistan or Iran might feel returning to his or her homeland?

2. What responsibilities do you think foreign countries have to help people affected by the conflict in Afghanistan?

Glossary

al-Qaeda A terrorist group based in the Middle East

asylum Protection or shelter from danger

democratic Describing a system of government in which people vote for the leaders who rule them

ethnic Describing a specific group that shares similarities such as customs or languages

extremist Having a strong belief in something; often political

hijab A head covering worn by some Muslim women

homeland The country where someone was born or grew up

host country A country that offers to give refugees a home

immigrants People who leave one country to live in another

internally displaced persons (IDPs) People who are forced from their homes during a conflict but remain in the country

invaded Entered by force

Islamic State in Iraq and the Levant Also called ISIL; a group of extremist Muslims who believe that people who do not share their beliefs are enemies

Islamophobia A fear or dislike of Muslims

ration card A card that allows refugees to pick up free food

refugees People who flee their country due to unsafe conditions

repatriation The voluntary process of a person returning to his or her homeland

rickshaw A two-wheeled vehicle pulled by a person

rights Privileges and freedoms protected by law

smuggler A person who moves people or things illegally

Soviet Union A former country in northern Europe that broke up in 1991

Taliban A terrorist group based in Afghanistan

terrorism The use of violence to force people to accept a point of view

trade A manual job that requires special training

Western Refers to the countries of western Europe, North America, and Australia

Learning More

Books

de Eulate, Ana A. *The Sky of Afghanistan*. Cuento de Luz SL, 2012.

Hunter, Nick. *Hoping for Peace in Afghanistan*. Gareth Stevens, 2012.

Winter, Jeanette. *Nasreen's Secret School: A True Story from Afghanistan*. Simon & Schuster, 2009.

Websites

kids.nationalgeographic.com/explore/countries/ afghanistan/#afghanistan-blue-mosque.jpg
Visit National Geographic Kids for a good overview of Afghanistan's geography and history.

www.timeforkids.com/destination/afghanistan/day-in-life
Read all about a day in the life of an Afghan boy.

www.trustineducation.org/why-afghanistan/afghanistan-the-basics
Visit this website for lots of facts about Afghanistan presented in a comparison table with the United States.

www.unicef.ca/sites/default/files/legacy/imce_uploads/images/ advocacy/co/crc_poster_en.pdf
Explore the United Nations Convention on the Rights of the Child.

Index

About the Author

In 1979 and 1980, Canada accepted 50,000 Vietnamese refugees. Helen Mason lived in a tiny Canadian community that hosted an extended family and an unaccompanied minor. She was one of many Canadians who helped provide household goods, and offered both friendship and a welcoming smile. This is her 34th book.